Nelson
ENGLISH

STUDENT BOOK 3

JOHN JACKMAN
WENDY WREN

Nelson

Contents

Language	Writing
adjectives with different meanings	planning a story – plot
there/their dictionary work (alphabetical order) 'or' words sentence punctuation	imaginative planning the plot
right/write adding 'ing' direct speech animal verbs	imaginative personal
antonyms dictionary work (alphabetical order)	instructions matching pictures and text personal preference lists
adverbs	story beginnings planning a story – when? descriptive imaginative
dictionary definitions direct speech verbs	limericks 'ew' pattern
number and colour adjectives comparative and superlative adjectives	plot/story structure finishing a story personal
words and pictures compound words singular and plural nouns	imaginative personal letter
compound words similes word families 'active' verbs 'being' verbs plurals of 'y' endings	imaginative descriptive
choosing adjectives	planning a story – setting descriptive book covers
dictionary definitions missing vowels punctuation marks contractions 'aw' pattern	paragraphs
synonyms direct speech parts of a sentence (subject/predicate)	imaginative conversations
abbreviations 'er' pattern	researching information imaginative personal
comparatives adding 'more' 'tion' suffix	punctuating conversations imaginative

UNIT 1

The Wooden Horse

The ancient Greeks fought many wars and had many heroes. One of the most famous wars was against the Trojans. Troy, where the Trojans lived, was a walled city ruled by King Priam. The Greeks built a camp outside the city. For ten years they tried to capture Troy. This is how the Greeks won the Trojan war.

Morning dawned over the windy plain of Troy, and the Trojans looked out towards the great camp of the Greeks which had stood there so long – looked, and rubbed their eyes and looked again.

'The Greeks have indeed gone!' they cried. 'The camp lies in ashes; there is not a man, not a ship to be seen. But there stands in the midst of the ruins a great Wooden Horse the like of which we have never seen.'

Then the gates of Troy were flung open and out poured young and old, laughing and shouting in their joy that the Greeks were gone at last. They came to the ruined camp and stood gazing at the great Wooden Horse.

At once a great argument broke out among the Trojans as to what should be done with the Horse. Some wanted to take it inside the city. Some wanted to fling it into the sea. It was decided to take the Wooden Horse into Troy. They dragged it across the plain but when they reached the gate of the city, the Horse proved too big to enter by it. The Trojans pulled down a section of the wall and brought it into the middle of Troy.

Night fell, and the Trojans feasted in their joy that the Great War was over and the Greeks had gone. At last, worn out with excitement and celebration, they fell asleep, leaving few guards by the walls and gates.

Inside the Horse the Greeks were sitting trembling and alert. When the first light of morning came they undid the bolt and opened the door in the Horse. They climbed down, crept through the silent streets, killed the sleepy guards and opened the gates to the armies of the Greeks who had sailed back to Troy in the dead of night!

Adapted from *The Tale of Troy* by Roger Lancelyn Green

Glossary

a *glossary* explains what a word means

midst means in the middle of

COMPREHENSION SKILLS

Read the passage and answer the questions.

1 Who was the King of Troy?

2 How do you think the Trojans felt when they saw that the Greeks had gone?

3 What did the Trojans do with the Wooden Horse?

4 Who was inside the Wooden Horse?

5 What did they do?

6 How do you think the Trojans felt when they woke up to find the Greeks inside the city?

LANGUAGE SKILLS

Different meanings

In the story the Greeks left a 'great Wooden Horse' outside the city of Troy.
Great is an adjective ('describing' word) with three meanings:

large　　very good　　important

1 Which meaning is the best for 'great Wooden Horse'?

2 Write three sentences of your own using the word **great** to show each meaning.

WRITING SKILLS

Planning a story

Before you begin to write a story you need to plan **what** is going to happen. This is called the **plot**.

Look at the **plot** of 'The Wooden Horse'.

Beginning
The Trojans wake up to find the Greek camp empty and a huge Wooden Horse left outside their city.

Middle
The Trojans talk about what they should do with the Horse. They bring it into the city and celebrate. When they go to sleep they do not guard the walls and gates very well.

End
The Greeks are inside the Horse.
Just before morning they come out of the Horse and capture the city of Troy.

Before you begin to write a story:

- you need to plan how your story begins.
- you need to plan what happens in the middle of your story.
- you need to plan how you are going to end your story.

The pictures below tell a story called 'The Big Bully'.

Beginning of the story

Middle of the story

End of the story

1 Write the **plot** of this story by saying what is happening in each picture.

2 Think about a story you could write called 'The Hide-out'. Write the **plot** of the story.

- How does your story begin?
- What happens in the middle of your story?
- How does your story end?

UNIT 2

The glory of Athens

Athens is a city in Greece. About 2000 years ago the people there worshipped the goddess of wisdom called Athena. They wanted to please Athena, so they built temples for her on a hill in the centre of their city. This area was called the Acropolis, which means 'high city'. The grandest temple on the Acropolis was the Parthenon. Many of its columns still stand today.

Most people did not go inside the Parthenon as people go into churches, temples or mosques today. They prayed outside. Inside was simply a huge statue of Athena made from gold and ivory.

The Acropolis was also a place for everyone to meet and enjoy themselves. There were many festivals and people would come in their best clothes. Sometimes there were sacrifices, which meant everyone had free meat to eat. This was a luxury because there was little space for people to keep farm animals in Athens.

Glossary

sacrifice means killing an animal for a god

luxury means expensive and enjoyable

COMPREHENSION SKILLS

A Copy these sentences. Fill in the missing words.

1 The hill in the centre of Athens was called the ______.

2 The people built ______ for the goddess Athena.

3 The grandest temple was the ______.

B Write a sentence to answer each question.

1 What was inside the Parthenon?

2 What was the Parthenon built for?

3 Why was it unusual for the people to eat meat in Athens?

LANGUAGE SKILLS

there and their

There usually means a place.
To help you remember, look for the smaller word 'here' in **there**. 'Here' also means a place.
Example: The temple is over **there**.
Their means 'belonging to them'. It is about people. In the middle of th**e**i**r** is 'i(I)' which is also to do with people.
Example: The Greeks were proud of **their** temples.

Is **there** or **their** missing from these sentences?

1 ______ were many beautiful temples in Athens.

2 The people built temples to please ______ goddess Athena.

3 ______ were many festivals.

4 "We like to go ______ with our parents," said the children.

5 One of ______ friends competed in the Olympic Games.

6 You can still see some remains of the Parthenon ______.

The words in your dictionary are in alphabetical order.
Words which begin with **a** come first,
next are **b** words, then **c** words,
and so on until the **z** words, which are last.

abcdefghijklmnopqrstuvwxyz

A Sort these words into alphabetical order.

1 **G**reece, **A**cropolis, **P**arthenon

2 **s**acrifice, **a**nimals, **t**emple

3 **f**estival, **i**vory, **g**old, **s**tatue, **c**olumns

There are lots of words which begin with the same letter. Dictionaries would be very difficult to use if the words were all jumbled together, so we need to look at the next letter as well. The following words have been sorted by looking at the second letters:
a**b**out, a**c**orn, a**d**d, a**e**roplane, after.

B Sort these groups of words into alphabetical order.
You will need to look at the second letters.

1 a**c**tor, a**b**le, a**e**roplane, a**d**der, a**f**raid

2 A**t**hens, A**c**ropolis, A**l**os, A**n**dros

3 d**r**ama, d**a**ncers, d**i**scus, D**e**lphi

4 m**y**th, m**e**tal, m**a**rble, m**o**saic

'or' pattern

How many **or** words can you find?
Play the game by bouncing around the square.
One word is done for you: c + **or** + k = c**or**k

c	h	th	f	h
st				w
m		**or**		ch
p				se
n	k	sh	t	y

1 Start in a small square. Write the letter down.

2 Bounce into the middle and write **or**.

3 Then bounce into another square to get the last letter.

Capital letters
Full stops
Question marks
Commas

We always begin a sentence with a **capital letter**. We usually end it with a **full stop** (**.**) or **question mark** (**?**). We use a **comma** (**,**) to separate each word in a list.
Example: The Greeks had many different gods including Athena, Zeus, Bacchus, Poseidon and Dionysus.

Write these sentences correctly.

1 the games were held in honour of Zeus

2 the first games were for men only

3 wrestling jumping archery and javelin were the main events

4 an olive branch was given to each of the winners

5 today men and women can take part

6 would you like to go to the Olympic Games

WRITING SKILLS

Write a story about the day you became a hero when you won a big race.
Plan the plot carefully before you begin.

UNIT 3

Today I ate...

... a special biscuit, a bowl of broth, and two cups of water... and yesterday I had nothing.

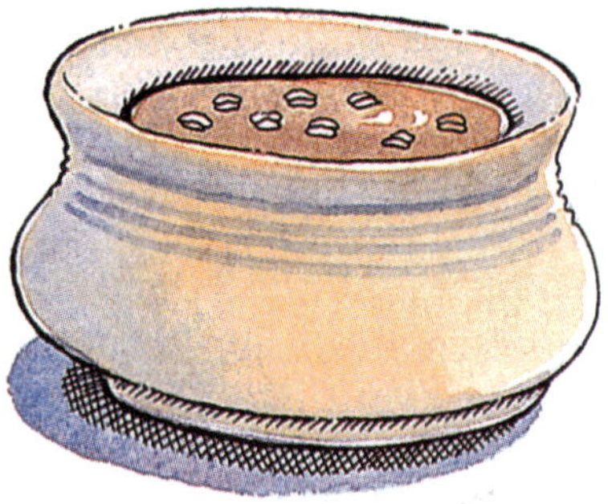

Most of us are lucky – we get food every day. Over half the people in the world are not so lucky. Many people have to go several days without any food. Their bodies use up the fat and they become thin. They feel weak and tired.

Many people cannot earn money to buy food and are too weak or ill to grow it themselves. In some countries they cannot grow food because there is not enough rain or because there is a war.

COMPREHENSION SKILLS

A Copy these sentences. Fill in the missing words.

1 Over ______ the people in the world do not have enough to eat.

2 If people do not have enough food their bodies become ______.

3 This makes them feel ______ and ______.

B Write a sentence to answer each question.

1 What is your favourite food?

2 Who buys your food?

3 Why do some people find it difficult to get food?

LANGUAGE SKILLS

right and write

Right can be used to mean several things, such as:

It is **right** to help hungry children.

Look **right** and left when crossing the road.

The bus went **right** to the school.

Write means to use letters or signs, usually on a piece of paper.

Choose **right** or **write** to finish these sentences.

1 It is not ______ that many people are hungry.

2 We should ______ to our government and ask them to give food to hungry children.

3 Fruit is on the left and vegetables are on the ______.

4 ______ neatly so that he can read your letter.

5 Is it ______ to show starving people on television?

Adding 'ing'

Remember, the vowels are a, e, i, o, u.

When you add **ing** to a very short word, look at the letter before the last letter. Is it a single vowel (a, e, i, o, u)?
If it is, double the last letter. Then add **ing**.
If it isn't, just add **ing**.
Examples:

bat, bat**ting**	shop, shop**ping**
sing, sing**ing**	read, read**ing**

This doesn't work for words ending in **w**, **x** or **y**.

A Add **ing** to these short words.

1 win	2 sit	3 hit	4 pat
5 get	6 slip	7 miss	8 spell
9 start	10 ask	11 wish	12 push

B Add **ing** to these short words. Some of the words end in **w**, **x** or **y**, so you just need to add **ing**.

1 box	2 fit	3 sow	4 try
5 mow	6 grow	7 fly	8 hiss

Direct speech
Inverted commas

Sometimes inverted commas are called 'speech marks'.

Sometimes we need to write the words that someone has spoken. This is called **direct speech**.

Direct speech should begin and end with **inverted commas** (" "). Inverted commas tell us when people have started to say something, and when they have finished.
Example: Naomi said, "I like fruit."

A Copy the words that the person said in each sentence.

1 The farmer said, "My crops won't grow because it hasn't rained for months."

2 Amrit said, "I like chicken and rice."

3 Mrs Okoye said, "We will plant beans and tomatoes in our school garden this year."

B Copy these sentences. Put inverted commas round the words that the person actually said.

1 James said, I like sweets.

2 Shall we have a picnic? asked Ruth.

3 Olu said, I like chips.

4 Would you like some fruit? asked Gran

The words **cluck** and **scratch** are verbs ('doing' words). They tell us what the hen does.

Make a list of as many farm animals as you can.

Now think of verbs to say what they do, how they eat and the noises they make, like this:

animal	**verb**
hen	clucks, scratches

WRITING SKILLS

What would you like to be?

If you could be a fruit or a vegetable what would you be?

1 Write about what you look like.
- Think about your colour, shape and size.
- Are you smooth or knobbly?
- Are you a bright colour, a dull colour or lots of colours?

2 Write about where you grow.
- Do you grow underground or above the ground?
- Do you grow on a tree?

3 Write about what happens to you after you are picked and before you are eaten.
- Are you peeled?
- Are you chopped or are you mashed?
- Are you cooked? How are you cooked?

UNIT 4

The Mad Hatter's tea party

Alice meets the Mad Hatter and the March Hare at a very odd tea party.

There was a table set out under a tree in front of the house, and the March Hare and the Hatter were having tea at it; a Dormouse was sitting between them, fast asleep, and the other two were using it as a cushion, resting their elbows on it, and talking over its head. "Very uncomfortable for the Dormouse," thought Alice; "only, as it's asleep, I suppose it doesn't mind."

The table was a large one, but the three were all crowded together at one corner of it. "No room! No room!" they cried out when they saw Alice coming.

"There's *plenty* of room!" said Alice indignantly, and she sat down in a large arm-chair at one end of the table.

"Have some wine," the March Hare said in an encouraging tone.

Alice looked all round the table, but there was nothing on it but tea. "I don't see any wine," she remarked.

"There isn't any," said the March Hare.

From *Alice in Wonderland* by Lewis Carroll

Glossary

indignantly means angrily

COMPREHENSION SKILLS

A Read the passage and answer the questions.

1 Where were the Mad Hatter and the March Hare having tea?

2 Where was the Dormouse?

3 What did the March Hare offer to Alice?

4 Why was this an odd thing to do?

5 What do you think Alice thought about the March Hare and his friends?

B The Mad Hatter's tea party wasn't much of a party. There was only tea to drink and no food! Write a list of food and drink you think the Mad Hatter should have had at his party.

LANGUAGE SKILLS

Antonyms

Antonyms are words with opposite meanings.
Examples: thick, thin comfortable, uncomfortable

A Which word in brackets is the antonym of these words?

1 rough (cold, smooth, heavy, hard)

2 large (dirty, full, big, small)

3 wide (narrow, fat, round, large)

4 fast (quick, speed, slow, follow)

Now write the words in sentences to show what they mean.

B Write **un** in front of these words.

1 dress	2 tie	3 fold	4 well
5 load	6 pack	7 happy	8 true

What happens to the meaning of the word? Write four of these new words in sentences to show what each means.

Dictionary work

Remember, we sort words into alphabetical order by looking at the **first** letter. If we have more than one word with the same first letter, we put these in order by looking at the **second** letter.

abcdefghijklmnopqrstuvwxyz

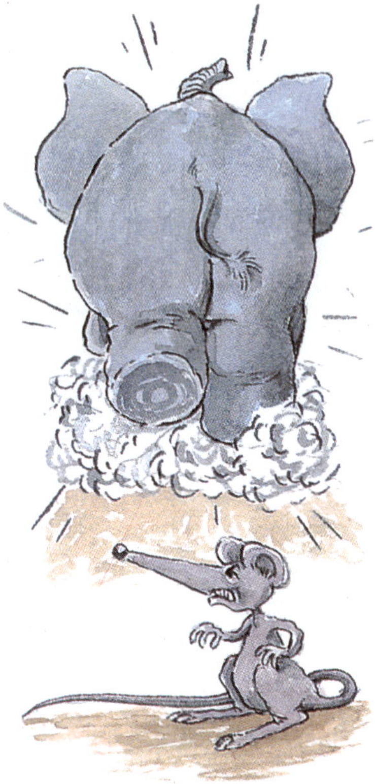

A Write these words in alphabetical order.

1 little, leaf, lamb

2 Alice, ant, Africa

3 mouse, meal, make, mice

4 elephant, escape, eat, enemy

B Now write these words in the order they appear in a dictionary.

1 grain, goat, house, hill

2 sheep, ox, hare, horse, owl

3 barn, high, hay, dip, bucket

WRITING SKILLS

Following instructions

1 Look at the pictures.
They show you how to make a jam sandwich.

The sentences that go with the pictures are muddled up.
Match the sentences with the pictures.
The first one is done for you.

a Get two slices of bread.

Put the two slices of bread together.
Put butter or margarine on each slice.
Cut the bread in half.
Get two slices of bread.
Cut each half in half again.
Put jam on one slice.

a b c

d

e

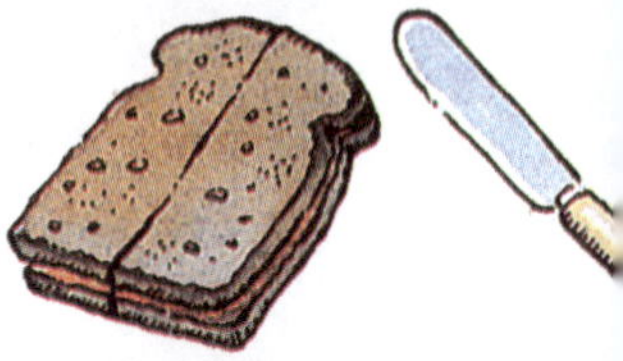

f

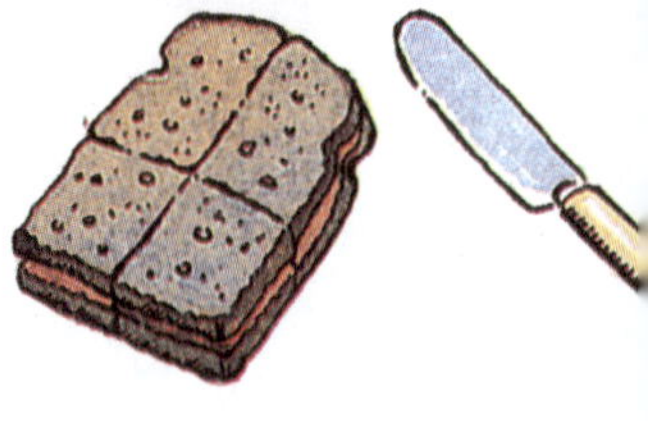

2 Write step-by-step instructions for one of these:
getting breakfast ready
making a cake for someone's birthday

A really horrible meal

Here is part of a poem by Michael Rosen called *Sulk*. It's about a child who doesn't like the food he has been asked to eat.
What do you think it might be?

> You know
> when you bite them
> there's all that slimy stuff;
> there are all those little lumpy bits
> in the slimy stuff
> and it all slides round your tongue
> and it all slides round your teeth.

Are there foods that you really hate?
Have you been asked to eat food that you thought would make you ill?

Write about what happened.

- Where were you?
- Did you get into trouble for not eating?
- Describe the food.
- Choose your words carefully as the poet did.

Make two lists, showing your most favourite and your least favourite foods.

UNIT 5

The Saga of Erik the Viking

The Vikings were very good at shipbuilding and sailing. They sailed to many lands including Russia, Britain and America. This is the beginning of a story called *The Saga of Erik the Viking*. Erik wanted to sail to a very unusual place.

This is a tale of a Viking warrior who lived hundreds and hundreds of years ago. His name was Erik. His ship was called Golden Dragon, and its figurehead was a fierce monster carved out of wood, and covered with gold leaf.

One day Erik said to his wife: ‘I must find the land where the sun goes at night.’ But his wife replied anxiously, ‘No one has ever been to that far country. And of those who have tried few have ever returned.’

‘You are right,’ said Erik bravely, ‘but, until I have sought that distant land, I shall never sleep in my bed again.’

So he called his son who was fifteen years old and told him he must guard their home carefully. Then he took his sword, which was called Blueblade, stepped on board Golden Dragon and sailed off towards the setting sun …

The next morning they found themselves alone on the ocean with great waves heaving the ship up and down. Erik looked up into the sky and smelt the wind.

‘We shan’t make it!’ Erik’s men whispered anxiously, one to the other, as the storm clouds blotted out the sun.

Terry Jones

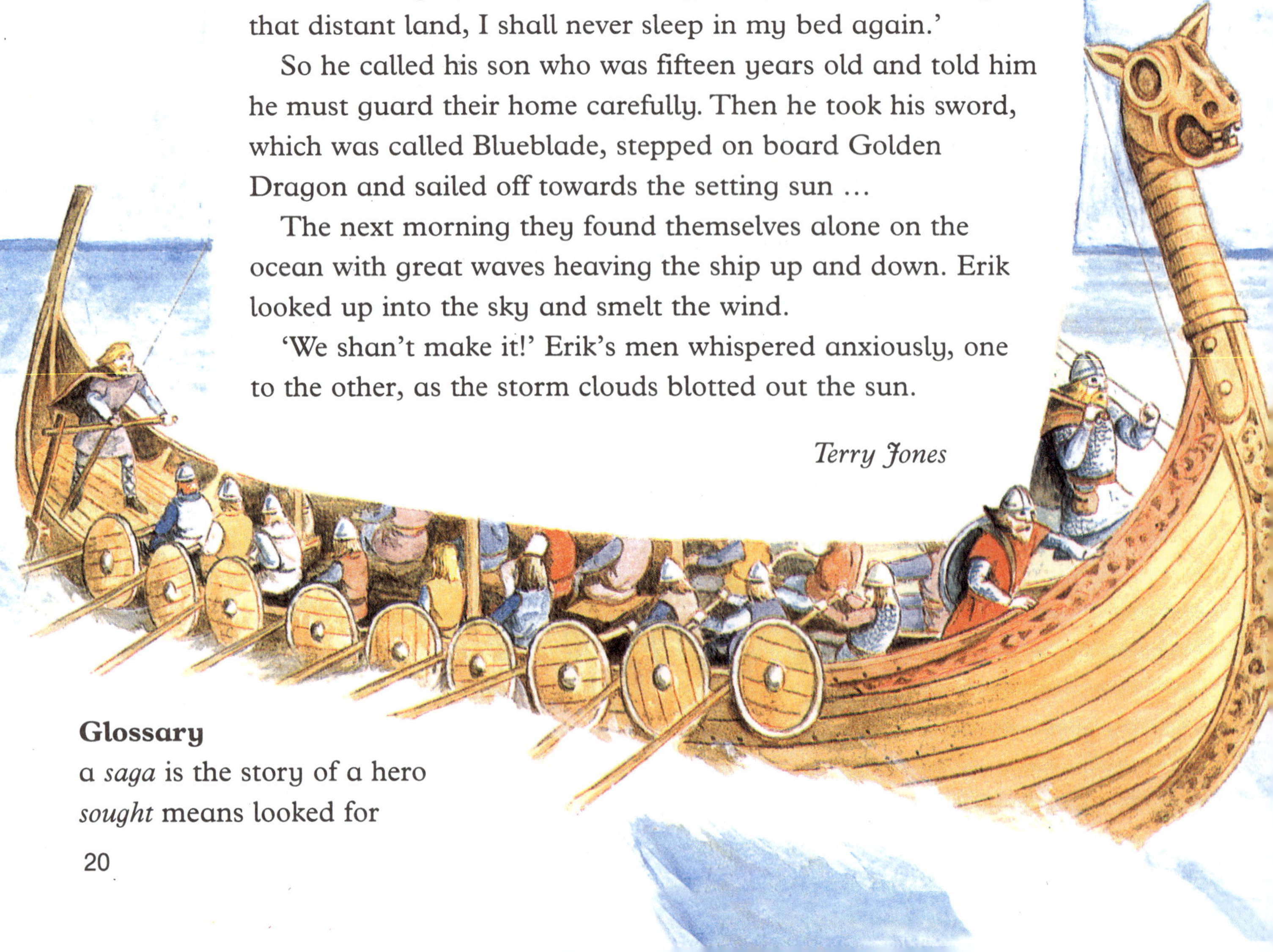

Glossary

a *saga* is the story of a hero
sought means looked for

COMPREHENSION SKILLS

Read the passage and answer the questions.

1 What do you think a warrior was?

2 Where on a ship would you find the figurehead?

3 How do you think that Erik's wife felt about Erik going on this journey?

4 Do you think that Erik would find 'the land where the sun goes at night'?

LANGUAGE SKILLS

Adverbs

An **ad**verb **adds** to the verb.

An **adverb** tells us more about *how, when,* or *where* the action of a verb took place.
Example: Erik's men whispered.
Erik's men whispered **anxiously**.
The **adverb** 'anxiously' describes how Erik's men whispered.
Many *how* adverbs end in **ly**.

A Copy these sentences. Underline the verbs and circle the adverbs. The adverbs tell us *how* the action took place.

1 Eric spoke bravely.

2 His wife replied anxiously.

3 They sailed quickly.

4 Erik's son guarded their home carefully.

B Copy these sentences.
Underline the verbs and circle the adverbs.
The adverbs show *when* or *where* the action took place.

1 They often sailed their ships.

2 Build the fire here.

3 Light it now.

4 Always wear the lucky ring.

5 Come home soon.

It's easy if you ask, "Which word tells me *when* or *where*?"

C Write five sentences with adverbs in them.
Underline the verbs and circle the adverbs.

WRITING SKILLS

Story beginnings

The beginning of a story sometimes tell us **when** the story happened.

The first sentence of *The Saga of Erik the Viking* tells us that the story happened a long time ago.

'This is a tale of a Viking warrior who lived **hundreds and hundreds of years ago**.'

1 There are lots of words and phrases that tell us when something happened.
Look at the pictures below.
Copy and finish the sentences by describing what is happening in the pictures.

a Early in the morning ...

b At night ...

c One beautiful summer day ...

d In the middle of Winter ...

2 Here are the beginnings of some other stories.
Write the words that tell you when the stories happened.

a Long ago there lived a man who had lots of cats.
b A few weeks ago there was a terrible storm.
c One day a stranger came to the village.

Planning a story

Before you write a story you need to plan **what** is going to happen.
You also need to plan **when** things happen in the story.

Think about a story you could write called 'The Accident'. Use these questions to help you plan when your story happened.

- Did the story happen a long time ago?
- Is it a modern story?
- Does everything happen in a day, a week, a month, or longer?
- Does the story happen in one season, or do the seasons change?

A Storm at Sea

Imagine you are one of Erik's sailors.
You are in the middle of the sea, far away from land, and a storm is coming.
Write about what happens.

- Remember to describe:
  the storm
  what you and the other sailors did
  what happened to the ship.
- Remember to write about **when** things happened.
  Think about when the storm started, how long it lasted and when it finished.

Viking expedition

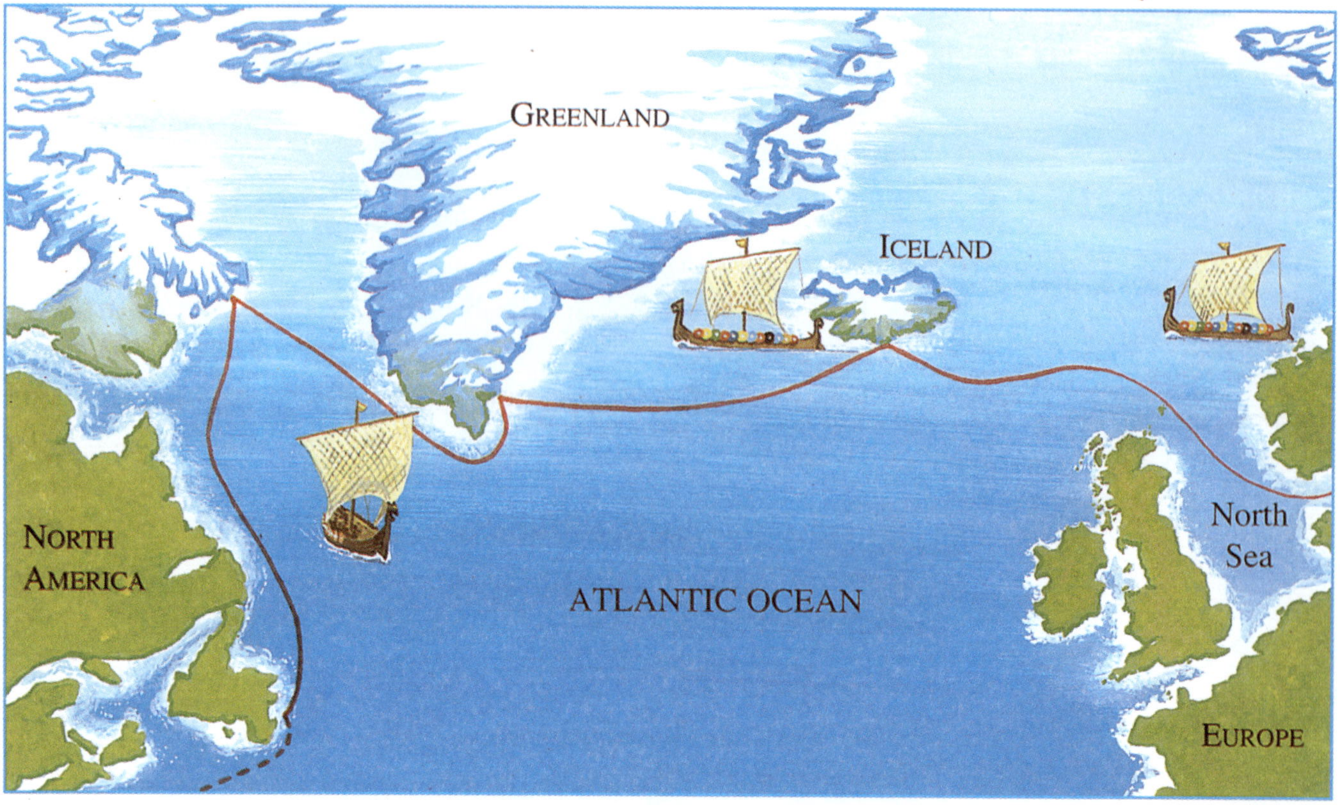

About 1000 years ago Viking sailors are thought to have been the first to discover Iceland, and some Viking families decided to stay there. Other sailors, like Erik the Red, sailed further west and found Greenland. Erik's son, Leif Eriksson, sailed on even further to a place that he called Vinland. Many people think that this was America.

On an expedition, the Vikings took tents and all the things they needed to survive when they first arrived. They had barrels full of salted meat and fish, and carried water and wine in leather skin bags. Soon they built houses, and villages and towns grew up. They began to trade with the local people, selling them skins, grain, cloth and slaves. They bought silk, glass, wine and, most important, metal to make their weapons.

COMPREHENSION SKILLS

A Copy these sentences. Fill in the missing words.

1 Erik the Red reached ______.

2 Erik's son was called ______.

3 The Vikings took ______ to live in when they landed.

B Write a sentence to answer each question.

1 What did Viking explorers carry with them?

2 How did the Viking invaders change a place when they settled there?

3 What was Leif Eriksson's name for America?

LANGUAGE SKILLS

Dictionary definitions

A dictionary is very useful for checking spellings. It also gives the meanings or **definitions** of words.

This is an entry in a dictionary.

noun ▼ *definition* ▼ *example* ▼

exhibition *n* a display: *an art exhibition*

Here are some more entries on the same page:

adjective ▼ *definition* ▼ *other words in the 'family'* ▼

expensive *adj* costing a lot. *opp* **inexpensive**

verb ▼ *definition* ▼

explain *v* to make the meaning of something clear. **explaining, explained.** ◀ *other words in the 'family'*

A Find these words in your dictionary. Write their definitions and say whether they are nouns, verbs or adjectives.

1 expert 2 explore 3 expedition 4 extraordinary

B Write your own sentences using the words **explore** and **expedition**.

Direct speech

Inverted commas or speech marks (“ ”) tell us when people are talking. *Example:* Leif said, **“Let’s land here.”**

The words inside the inverted commas are treated as a smaller sentence inside a bigger sentence. These words start with a **capital letter** and end with a **full stop** or **question mark**.

However, sometimes the words that are said come first. In this case the words have a **comma**, instead of a full stop, at the end. *Example:* **“Let’s land here,”** said Leif.

A Write these sentences.
Add the inverted commas.

1 Harold said, I’m getting tired.

2 Ingrid asked, How much further do we have to go?

3 I think I can see land, said Leif.

4 Where? said Ingrid excitedly.

5 Keep rowing and we’ll land before dark, said Leif encouragingly.

B Copy these sentences and add all the missing inverted commas, commas and full stops.

1 The Viking leader said We are going to set up camp in Iceland

2 It will take us a week to get there said the captain

3 It is too rough to sail in this weather said the sailors

4 Be brave and trust me said the captain

Verbs

A **verb** is an active or 'doing' word.
It tells us what is being done in a sentence.
Example: The Vikings **sail** the ship.

Copy these word webs. Find verbs in the box which go with the nouns. Four verbs have been done for you.

trickles	paddles	ploughs	sows
sails	blazes	plants	drips
sprinkles	rows	smoulders	floods
harvests	navigates	sparks	burns

1 trickles — **water**

2 ploughs — **farmer**

3 rows — **sailor**

4 burns — **fire**

WRITING SKILLS

Limericks

Limericks are short, funny rhymes with five lines.
Can you see which lines rhyme with each other?

There was an old Viking I k**new**
Who loved his cabbage and st**ew**.
So when they ran out
He gave a great shout
And cried, "What else can I ch**ew**?"

Finish this limerick with **ew** rhyming words. Your limerick should have five lines. The first, second and fifth lines should rhyme with each other, and the third and fourth lines should rhyme. The words in the box may help.

There was an old man I ________
Who …

stew	few	knew	dew	chew	nephew	
grew	drew	new	threw	flew	blew	view

UNIT 7

Journeys

People have always needed to go on journeys, so bridges have been built for thousands of years. The first were very simple, like a log or a large slab of stone across a stream.

Some of the longest, modern road bridges over rivers are suspension bridges. They are made from steel cables. Two large towers are built and the steel cables are hung between them. More cables hang down from the main cables and these 'suspend' the road. This is why these bridges are called 'suspension' bridges. The road is high enough for boats to pass underneath.

Engineers need to be very careful. If the design of the suspension bridge is not exactly right, it can start to twist and turn in a high wind. This happened to the Tacoma Narrows Bridge in the USA, which shook itself to pieces.

The Humber Bridge in Britain has the longest span in the world. Its main span is 1410 metres across. An even bigger bridge is being built in Japan. Its main span will be 1990 metres.

COMPREHENSION SKILLS

A Copy these sentences. Fill in the missing words.

1 The simplest bridge is a ______ or a slab of stone.

2 On a suspension bridge the cables are made of ______.

3 The ______ Bridge is the longest suspension bridge.

B Write a sentence to answer each question.

1 In which country is the longest suspension bridge being built?

2 What are the main steel cables hung between?

3 What happened to Tacoma Narrows Bridge?

LANGUAGE SKILLS

Numbers and colours

Numbers and colours can be adjectives (describing words).
Number adjectives describe the *number* of nouns.
Example: There are **two** bridges.
They can also describe the *order* of nouns.
Example: This is the **second** bridge.

Colour adjectives describe the colour of nouns.
Example: We walked across the **red** bridge.

A Write the order words that go with these numbers.

number	two	one	seven	ten	three
order	second				

B Write five sentences about this picture.
Each sentence must have a colour adjective in it.

Comparative and superlative adjectives

An adjective is a 'describing' word. We use a **comparative** adjective when we compare two things.
To make a comparative adjective we add **er**, or **ier** if there is a letter **y**.
Example: This bridge is long**er** than that one.

We use a **superlative** adjective when we compare three or more things. To make a superlative adjective we add **est**, or **iest** if there is a letter **y**.
Examples: The Humber Bridge is the long**est** bridge in the world. It is closed on the wind**iest** days in the year.

adjective	**comparative**	**superlative**
long	long**er**	long**est**
old	old**er**	old**est**
busy	bus**ier**	bus**iest**
windy	wind**ier**	wind**iest**

Notice what happens to the letter **y**.

A Choose a comparative or superlative adjective from the tinted box above for these sentences.

1 The bridge over the river is o_______ than the bridge over the railway.

2 The b_______ day on the bridge is Friday.

3 The Humber Bridge in Britain is the l_______ suspension bridge in the world.

4 It is w_______ today than it was yesterday.

B Copy and complete the table below.

adjective	**comparative**	**superlative**
long	longer	longest
slow	___	___
high	___	___
happy	___	___
small	___	___
pretty	___	___

WRITING SKILLS

A special journey

1

2

3

4

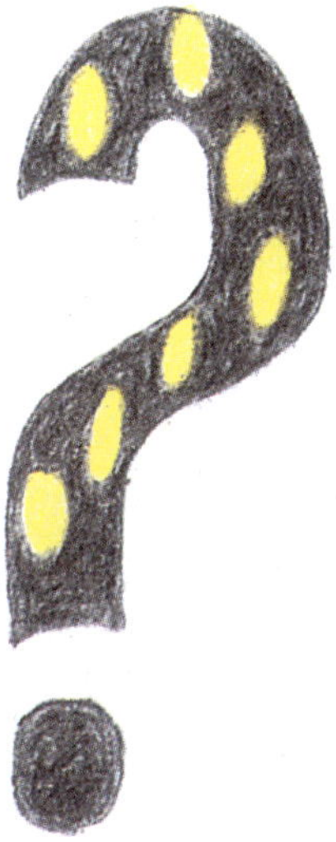

1 Write a sentence for each picture saying what the family is doing. Imagine what might happen in picture 4.

When you have finished you will have written what has happened in the story. This is the plot of a story about the family going on a special journey.

2 Write about a journey you have made. Think about the plot before you start.

Check-up I

VOCABULARY

A Choose one of the words in brackets to fill in the gaps.

1 ______ will be games at my party. (there, their)

2 They left ______ muddy boots outside. (there, their)

3 The ball landed over ______. (there, their)

4 I always try to ______ neatly. (write, right)

5 Turn ______ at the end of the road. (write, right)

6 She always thinks he is ______. (write, right)

B Which word in brackets is the antonym?

1 large (under, small, in, dirty) = small

2 smooth (heavy, slippery, rough, gentle)

3 slow (runner, fast, old, big)

4 inside (on, over, outside, top)

C Copy and complete the table. Fill in the missing adjectives.

adjective	comparative	superlative
big	bigger	biggest
______	shorter	______
______	______	smallest
long	______	______
______	prettier	______
funny	______	______
______	older	______
______	______	heaviest
kind	______	______
______	______	saddest

PUNCTUATION AND GRAMMAR

A Add capital letters, full stops and question marks to the sentences.

1 i like my kitten 2 she is black and white
3 her name is paddy 4 do you have a pet

B Add capital letters, commas, question marks and full stops to the sentences.

1 can i have a birthday party
2 we will need to buy some cakes biscuits and snacks
3 can peter anna ali kim and musa come to my party

C Add inverted commas (speech marks) to the sentences.

1 That was a really brilliant party, said Ali.
2 Thanks for inviting us, added Peter and Anna.
3 Musa said, will you come to my party next week?

D A verb is an 'active' word. Adverbs tell us *how, when* or *where* the action is happening. Underline the verbs and circle the adverbs.

1 The children ran home quickly.
2 The cat purred gently.
3 I fell heavily and hurt my knee.
4 Cross the road here.
5 "You always win," said Florence.

SPELLING

A Add **ing** to these. You may need to double the last letter.

1 jump	2 get	3 put	4 wish
5 push	6 sit	7 pat	8 fall

B Put these words in alphabetical order.

1 Tom, Amina, Olu, Yin 2 cup, chair, car, clock
3 apple, bath, dog, actor 4 want, word, wise, Wesley

Aztecs

The Aztecs lived in Mexico about five hundred years ago. They did not have an alphabet but wrote in pictures, called 'glyphs'. Some glyphs were pictures of objects to give the idea of an action, like 'war' or 'travel'. Some words were difficult to draw, so they drew glyphs of the sounds of the word. They were not exact, but everyone knew what they meant.

Their city of Quauhtitlan was written like this:

The first part of the name of the city was **Quauh** which is close to the sound for 'tree' (**quauitl**):

The last part of the name of the city was **titlan** which is close to the sound for 'teeth' (**tlantli**):

 =  + 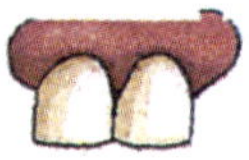

The Aztecs also wrote numbers using glyphs.

1 to 19 were shown by fingers:

20 was shown by a flag:

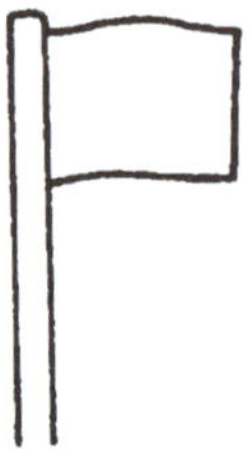

400 was shown by a feather:

COMPREHENSION SKILLS

A Copy these sentences. Fill in the missing words or numbers.

1 The ______ did not have an alphabet.

2 They wrote in pictures which were called ______.

3 This glyph  shows number ______.

B Write a sentence to answer each question.

1 What is a glyph?

2 How did the Aztecs write Quauhtitlan?

3 How might they have written 420?

LANGUAGE SKILLS

Words and pictures

Make your own glyphs for these words.

1 foot	2 cup	3 rain
4 ball	5 tooth	6 coat

Compound words

Only draw one raincoat in the last glyph.

Make glyphs for these compound words.
Compound words are two smaller words joined together.

1 cupboard 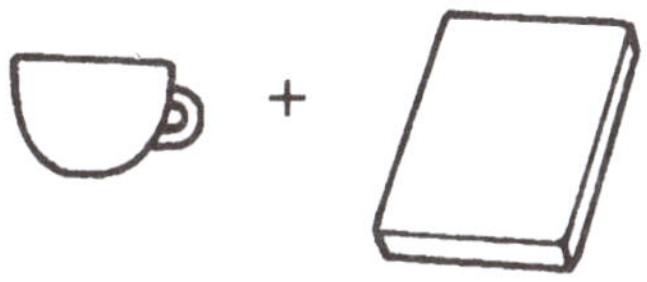 = cupboard

2 toothbrush

3 armchair

4 three footballs

5 20 raincoats

Singular and plural nouns

Adding 's'

'Glyph' is **singular**. We mean only one glyph.
'Glyphs' is **plural**. We mean more than one glyph.
We add **s** to show that we mean more than one.

A Copy these words. Add **s** to make the plural of each.

1 one glyph, two glyphs

2 one feather, two ______

3 one finger, two ______

4 one rope, two ______

5 one fan, two ______

6 one boat, two ______

We need to add **es** to some nouns to make them plural.
These are the nouns that end with **s, x, ch** or **sh**.

B Write the plurals for these nouns.

1 bus

2 dish

3 box

4 hatch

5 fish

6 arch

7 church

8 torch

C Add **s** or **es** to each of these words to make them plural.

stream	field	wish	glass	fox	torch
span	match	cart	step	rock	grass

WRITING SKILLS

The Aztecs

The Aztecs ruled in central and southern Mexico from 1325 to 1521 when the Spaniard Hernán Cortés landed in Mexico.

When Cortés and his men arrived in Mexico in 1519 they were met by the Aztecs who rowed out to the Spanish ships. The Spaniards asked them who they were and who their king was. They answered, "Lords, we come from Mexico and our king is Montezuma." Cortés was soon to hear a lot about the fierce and powerful Aztec king. The Spanish and the Aztecs then gave each other gifts. The Aztecs gave beautiful embroidered cloth and the Spanish gave glass beads.

The Aztecs left and travelled quickly to tell their king about the strangers. They showed him the presents that Cortés had given them and also drawings they had done of the Spanish ships, guns, horses and armour.

Writing a letter

Imagine you are Cortés the Spanish sailor.
You have just met the Aztecs for the first time.
Write a letter home telling your family about the Aztecs.
Remember you have just landed in a strange country.

- How were the Aztecs dressed? (The picture will help you.)
- What did they say and do? (Remember about the gifts.)
- What did you think about them?
- Are you surprised that the Aztecs are friendly?
- Did you think they would attack you?
- What do you think about their gift?
- Are you looking forward to meeting the Aztec king?

UNIT 9

White Cat in Moonlight

Through moonlight's milk
She slowly passes
As soft as silk
Between tall grasses.
I watch her go
So sleek and white,
As white as snow,
The moon so bright
I hardly know
White moon, white fur –
Which is the light
And which is her.

Douglas Gibbon

COMPREHENSION SKILLS

A Copy these sentences. Fill in the missing words.

1 The cat passes between tall _______.

2 She was _______ and white.

3 The colour of the moon was _______.

B Copy the sentences that are true.

1 It was difficult to see the black cat in the dark.

2 The cat was sleek and white.

3 The night was dark and cloudy.

4 The moon shone brightly.

LANGUAGE SKILLS

Compound words

Take one word from each box to make a compound word. Remember, a compound word is when two other words are joined together.

Like this: moon + light = moonlight

up	after
screw	sea
pine	thunder
home	tooth

set	ache
work	storm
noon	apple
weed	driver

Similes

Similes describe something by comparing it to something similar. They often begin with **as** or **like**.

Example: She slowly passes
As soft as silk

A Copy these sentences and neatly underline the similes.

1 The cat was sleek and white, as soft as snow.

2 The moon was like a big round dish.

B Make up your own sentences using these similes.

as clear as crystal

as quiet as a mouse

as fierce as a lion

Word families

Find four word families in the box.
Like this: 1 slow, slowly, slower, slowest

explore	agree	explorer	quick
quicker	quickly	discover	explored
discovery	agreement	quickest	agreeable
discovered	discovering	agreed	exploring

'Active' verbs

Copy these sentences and underline the verbs.
Remember, most verbs are active or 'doing' words.
They tell us what is being done in a sentence.

1 I watch her go.

2 She creeps through the grass.

3 I sit on a rock.

4 I walk home.

'Being' verbs

Most verbs are active or 'doing' verbs,
but verbs can also be about **'being'**. These verbs are
am, **is**, **are**, **was**, **were**, **will be**, and **to be**.
Example: The air **is** cold.

A Use a different 'being' verb in each sentence.

1 The air _______ cold.

2 I _______ cold.

3 It _______ _______ dark soon.

4 My friend _______ here last night.

5 They _______ scared of the dark.

6 I used _______ _______ scared, but I'm not any more!

B Write five sentences, each with a different 'being' verb.

Plurals
'y' endings

Remember
the vowels:
a, e, i, o, u.

We need to add **ies** to some nouns to make them plural.
You will spot these nouns because they end with **y**.
Example: one stor**y**, two stor**ies**
But if the letter in front of the **y** is a vowel, simply add **s**.
Examples: **toy** toy**s**, **day** day**s**

A Change these words into plurals.

1 toy 2 boy 3 bay
4 valley 5 alley 6 donkey

B Now change these words into plurals.

1 day 2 jay 3 fly 4 pony
5 monkey 6 story 7 activity 8 jockey
9 trolley 10 way 11 baby 12 berry

WRITING SKILLS

Read the poem on page 38 again.
Imagine that while you are watching the cat you slowly start to shrink and become just 3 centimetres tall! The grass towers high above your head.

Suddenly, all the creatures in the grass seem huge, but they are friendly and can talk to you.

When you get home you write about what happened.
Remember to write about:

- how you felt as you shrunk
- what the cat looked and sounded like
- what you talked about to the other creatures.

UNIT 10

Castles

The fisherman and his wife

One day a poor fisherman catches a magic fish. The fisherman's wife wants to live in a stone castle and the magic fish makes the wish come true.

The fisherman and his wife went to the castle that the magic fish had given them to live in. It was a huge, stone castle with ivy growing up the walls. There were a lot of servants and a lot of rooms. All the rooms had beautiful furniture. The chairs and tables were made of gold. Behind the castle there was a lovely garden and a huge wood. They saw sheep, goats, hares and deer. In the castle courtyard there were stables and cow houses. It really was a wonderful place.

Glossary

courtyard means a space with buildings around it

COMPREHENSION SKILLS

A Read about the fisherman and answer the questions.

1 What did the castle look like from the outside?

2 What was in the rooms of the castle?

3 What did the furniture look like?

4 What was behind the castle?

Not all castles in traditional tales are quite so wonderful as the fisherman's castle.

The Snow Queen

Gerda is looking for her brother Kay. He has been taken away by the wicked Snow Queen. While Gerda is looking for him she is captured by some robbers and taken to their castle.

Suddenly the carriage stopped. They had reached the courtyard of the robbers' castle. Its walls were cracked from top to bottom. Crows and ravens were flying out of the gaps and holes. Huge hounds, each one looking as if he could swallow a man, leapt high into the air, but not a single bark came from them, for that was forbidden. In the great old hall, cobwebbed and black with soot, a large fire burnt on the stone floor. The smoke drifted about under the roof, trying to find its way out. A vast cauldron of soup was bubbling away. Hares and rabbits were roasting on turning-spits.

Adapted from *The Snow Queen* by Hans Christian Andersen, translated by Naomi Lewis

Glossary

forbidden means not allowed
vast means very big

B Read *The Snow Queen* passage and answer the questions.

1 What words and phrases describe the castle?

2 Write a list of things inside the castle.

LANGUAGE SKILLS

Choosing adjectives

In the fisherman's castle there is **beautiful** furniture and a **lovely** garden.
In the robbers' castle there is a **large** fire and a **vast** cauldron.
Beautiful and **lovely** mean nice to look at.
Large and **vast** mean very big.

Look at the adjectives in the box.

huge	cute	massive	pretty
handsome	attractive	enormous	gigantic

1 Make a list of the adjectives that mean nice to look at.

2 Make a list of the adjectives that mean very big.

3 Use two 'nice to look at' words in sentences of your own.

4 Use two 'very big' words in sentences of your own.

WRITING SKILLS

Where does it happen?

Before you begin to write a story you need to plan **where** the story happens.
This is called the **setting**.

The **setting** for part of 'The fisherman and his wife' is a stone castle with beautiful furniture, a lovely garden and a huge wood.
The **setting** for part of 'The Snow Queen' is an old castle with a cobwebbed, black hall which is very smoky.

Think about a story you could write called 'Trapped'.
Think about the **setting** for your story.

- Where are you trapped?
  It could be in a castle under attack, a tunnel, or a crashed car.
  You may have a better idea!
- What sort of things are there around you.

Write a list of words and phrases that describe where you are.

Looking at book covers

Here are the front covers of five story books.
Write one or two sentences to describe the setting for each story.

4

5

UNIT 11

The Chinese princess

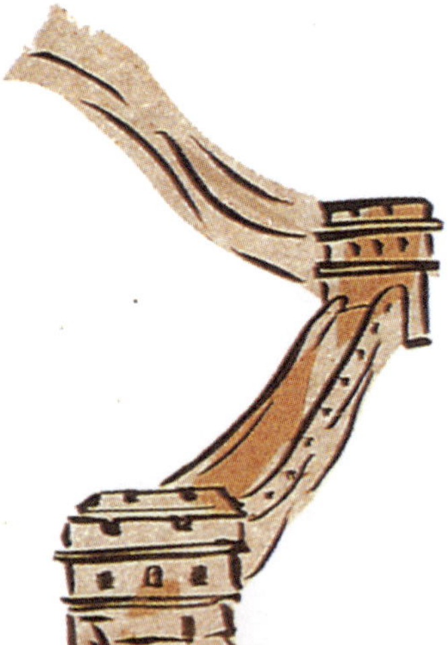

The princess gazed up sadly at the Emperor of China's Great Wall. This was where her husband had been forced to work. He had died here, in the hot sun, crushed beneath a pile of falling rocks. She had heard awful stories about the wall. Hundreds had died as they worked. The wall had been built over the bodies where they fell.

How was she ever going to find her husband's body if it was sprawled under masses of rock? She wanted to take his body away and bury it herself.

Suddenly she saw something at her side. A friendly spirit curled out of the bushes. "Princess," it said, "I have come to help you. First cut your finger and then hold it out in front of you. The drops of blood will lead to your husband." With that, the spirit vanished.

She took a thorn and pricked her finger. Drops of blood splashed down on the ground. She followed the spots to the wall. The princess was overcome with joy and sorrow. As the spirit had promised, the trail had drawn her to the body of her husband.

This Chinese legend is a very old story. The Emperor Shih Huang Ti gave orders for the building of the Great Wall of China over 2000 years ago. It was to be a huge wall to keep out all his enemies.

Adapted from *A Beautiful Legend* by Richard Worsnop

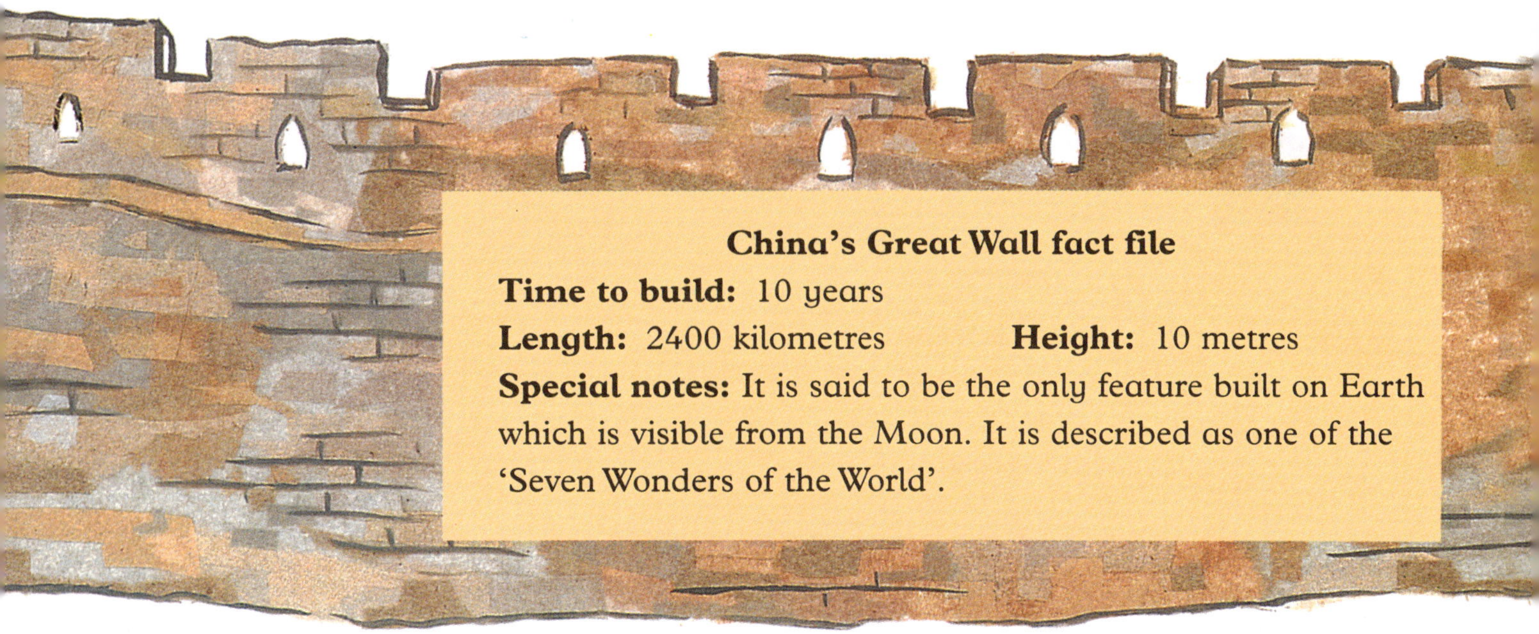

China's Great Wall fact file

Time to build: 10 years

Length: 2400 kilometres **Height:** 10 metres

Special notes: It is said to be the only feature built on Earth which is visible from the Moon. It is described as one of the 'Seven Wonders of the World'.

COMPREHENSION SKILLS

A Copy these sentences. Fill in the missing words.

1 The princess was sad because her husband was ______.

2 A ______ helped her to find his body.

3 She followed the drops of ______ from her finger.

B Write a sentence to answer each question.

1 When was the Great Wall of China built?

2 Why was it built?

3 Do you think the story of the sad princess is true?

LANGUAGE SKILLS

Dictionary definitions

A Find these words in the story. Imagine you were making a dictionary, and write a definition for each one. Remember, a definition is the meaning of a word.

overcome awful sorrow legend aware

B Now look up each word in your dictionary and write the dictionary definition. Is it similar to your definition?

Missing vowels

Can you see what is missing in this sentence?

My tchr mks m wrk t hrd.

Yes, all the vowels have been left out.

Write a note to a friend leaving out the vowels.
Your friend must reply to show that it has been understood.

Punctuation marks

Remember to use capital letters, full stops, question marks and inverted commas.

All the punctuation marks have been left out of these sentences. Write them correctly.

1 the legend is about a sad princess

2 shih huang ti was a cruel emperor

3 he ruled china for many years

4 i will help you said the kind spirit

5 why is the emperor so unkind she asked

Contractions

Contractions are used in place of two words.
Examples: **It's** is a contraction for **it is.**
Don't is a contraction for **do not**.
The words are made smaller by leaving out some letters and putting in an apostrophe (') in their place.

In your book write the contractions in these sentences.
Next to each contraction write the words which it replaces.

1 The princess didn't know what to do.

2 "I can't bear to think of him buried there," she said.

3 They shouldn't be so cruel.

4 "I'll help you," said the spirit.

5 "I won't ever come here again," cried the princess.

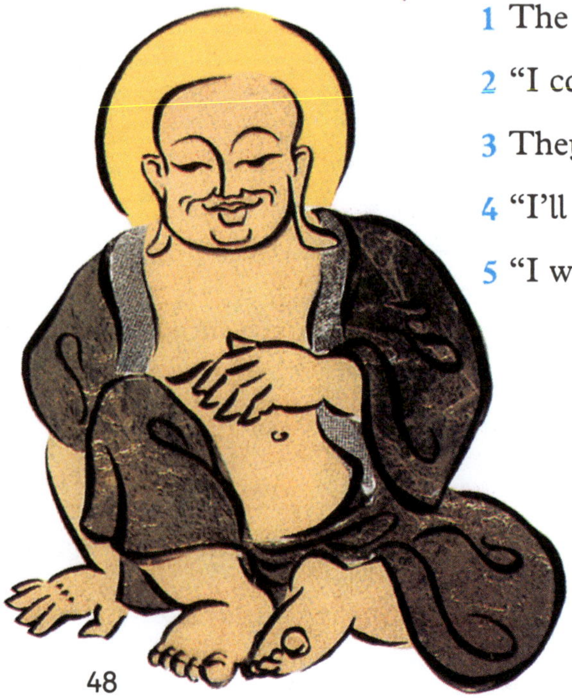

‘aw’ pattern

The **aw** pattern can be at the beginning of a word (**awful**),
or in the middle of a word (spr**awl**ed),
or at the end of a word (s**aw**).

1 Write all the **aw** words in the story.

2 Write all the **aw** words hidden in this wordsearch.
The words are across and down.

b	z	s	p	r	a	w	l
w	a	w	a	y	p	p	a
l	d	a	q	c	l	a	w
h	a	w	t	h	o	r	n
a	w	a	r	e	q	p	j
w	n	k	r	a	w	a	a
k	s	e	e	s	a	w	w

WRITING SKILLS

Paragraphs

A **paragraph** is a group of sentences about one main idea. To show our reader when a new **paragraph** is beginning we start a new line. A **paragraph** should have sentences about the same subject.

A Look at the story again and answer these questions.

1 How many paragraphs has the writer used?

2 Is the first paragraph a good start to the story?

3 Does the last paragraph finish the story?

4 Do all the paragraphs have the same number of sentences?

B Find a story you have written, or choose one from a book. Answer the same questions about your story or piece of writing.

UNIT 12

Living things breathe

All animals must have air to live. Air is a mixture of many gases. The most important gas for breathing is oxygen.

We breathe air through our noses. It goes down a tube, called the windpipe, into our lungs. Our lungs are two large, spongy bags in our chest. We can see our chests get bigger as we breathe air in.

Our lungs help oxygen in the air get into our blood. The oxygen then goes with the blood to all parts of our body. People going to places where there may not be enough oxygen must take it with them in tanks.

Most big animals get oxygen through their lungs as well, but some small animals breathe in other ways.

Earthworms take in oxygen through their thin skin. Slugs and snails have a large hole in their sides and insects have many tiny holes to breathe through.

Water creatures have other ways of breathing. A water beetle comes to the surface and puts the tip of its tail out into the air. It then takes a bubble of air under the water. It breathes the air in the bubble through little tubes in its tail.

Fishes get their oxygen from air which is in the water. A fish uses its gills to take oxygen out of the water. You can see the air in water, when water is heated in a saucepan and it bubbles.

COMPREHENSION SKILLS

A Copy these sentences. Fill in the missing words.

1 The most important gas we breathe is ______.

2 We breathe air through our ______.

3 Insects breathe through tiny ______ in their sides.

B Write a sentence to answer each question.

1 How is the oxygen passed around our body?

2 How do slugs breathe?

3 How can we see that there is air in water?

LANGUAGE SKILLS

Synonyms

Words that mean the same, or nearly the same, are called **synonyms**.
Examples: large, big   strong, powerful

A Find the synonyms in the box.

tiny	enough	small	under	maybe	heat
break	shout	perhaps	warm	beneath	
get	obtain	sufficient	yell	smash	

B Write a sentence for three of the synonyms you have found to show they mean the same. Like this:

1 We (**obtain/get**) oxygen from the air.

Direct speech

Words such as **The firefighter said**, or **I shouted**, tell us who is speaking. These words may come before, in the middle of, or at the end of words actually spoken.

If the spoken words are separated, we don't need a capital letter for the second part. This is because it is still part of the same sentence.

Examples:
The firefighter said, "This smoke is so thick it is hard to breathe."
"This smoke is so thick," **the firefighter said**, "it is hard to breathe."
"This smoke is so thick it is hard to breathe," **said the firefighter**.

A Copy the words that are actually spoken in these sentences.

1 The air, panted the climber, is very thin up here.

2 Please help, cried the woman, he is not breathing properly!

3 Swimming underwater, said the diver, is an amazing thing to do.

4 All I hope, said the astronaut, is that this spacesuit doesn't leak.

B Now write the whole of these sentences, putting in inverted commas.

Parts of a sentence

All sentences begin with a capital letter and end with a full stop.

A simple sentence has two parts.
The **subject** is the thing or person written about.
The **predicate** is the rest of the sentence.
It includes the verb, and it tells us what is happening.
Example: A water beetle breathes through its tail.
subject *predicate*

A Make simple sentences from these subjects and predicates.

subject	**predicate**
Fishes	have two lungs.
Earthworms	have a shell.
Humans	breathe through their skin.
Snails	breathe through gills.

B Copy these sentences. Then divide them into subjects and predicates. Draw a neat line under the verbs. Like this:

1 Earthworms / take in oxygen through their skin.

2 Snails collect air through their sides.

3 Astronauts carry oxygen tanks on spacewalks.

4 Humans breathe air through their noses.

5 The water beetle collects an air bubble.

WRITING SKILLS

Fire! Fire!

Imagine you and a friend are walking in the countryside when you see smoke billowing up from beyond some trees. To your horror, you realise that the dry grass and bushes are burning fiercely. You rush back to the village to warn everyone, and to get help. But the village is deserted! Everyone has gone to market.

Write the conversation that takes place between you and your friend.

- Make a plan before you start.
- Make it interesting and exciting to read.
- Try not to use the word ‘then’.
- Try to think of better words than ‘said’ if you can.

Mother Teresa of Calcutta

Have you ever wondered what it would be like to be famous? Some people dream that one day they will be great swimmers, footballers or athletes. Others have hopes of becoming rich musicians or film stars, and some people would even like to be President or Prime Minister. Every now and then, someone becomes famous just for helping other people. One famous person like this is Mother Teresa.

Mother Teresa came from Albania, a very poor country, and went to India as a nun. Although some people in India are rich, she realised that many still live in terrible poverty. This made her sad and she knew she must try to help, so she started a group of nuns called the Missionaries of Charity.

Mother Teresa and the nuns who help her have now opened over fifty homes for orphan children, and in many other places they feed and care for the very poor who are too old or sick to help themselves. They are opening more homes whenever they can.

COMPREHENSION SKILLS

A Copy these sentences. Fill in the missing words.

1 Mother Teresa came from ______.

2 She went to ______.

3 She was very upset to see so many ______ people.

B Write a sentence to answer each question.

1 What is Mother Teresa's organisation called?

2 What does it try to do?

3 If you could be famous, what would you like to be known for?

LANGUAGE SKILLS

Abbreviations

Abbreviations are short forms of words.
Example: Nuns are often called 'Sisters'. If you were to write to a nun you would write **Sr** in front of her name on the envelope. **Sr** is an abbreviation for Sister.

Write these lists in your book. Use a ruler to draw lines to link each abbreviation with its meaning.

abbreviation	meaning
Sr	minute
Mr	kilometre
km	Prime Minister
Rd	Road
Dr	Sister
m	Doctor
min	Mister
PM	metre
UN	Street
St	United Nations

'er' pattern

Look
Cover
Remember
Write
Check

The **er** pattern usually comes at the end of a word.
Look carefully at these words. Now cover them.
Ask a friend to check how many you can spell correctly.
Try again if you get some wrong.

mother	river	under	letter
father	water	over	pattern
brother	silver	ever	person
sister	finger	after	

Adding 'er'

We usually double the last letter if the one before it is a single vowel (a, e, i, o, u).

The **er** pattern is sometimes added to words to make a new word, such as 'bigger'.
Do you see what else has happened?
Often when we add **er** to a small word we must double the last letter before adding **er**.

Copy and complete this table.

big	bigger
swim	
mad	madder
win	
sad	
fit	fitter
hot	
run	runner

WRITING SKILLS

Finding information

People are famous for lots of different things.
Look at this list:

Mao Tse Tung

Queen Elizabeth II

Elvis Presley

Charles Dickens

Shakespeare

Margaret Thatcher

Carl Lewis

Mother Teresa

Walt Disney

Nelson Mandela

Copy the list into your book and next to each name write what they are or were famous for.
Where will you find the information you need if you do not know?

If I were famous ...

Imagine you are a famous person.
Write about what you are famous for.

- Did you invent something?
- Were you the first person to do something?
- Are you better than anyone else at doing something?
- Do you like being famous?
- What is bad about being well known?

UNIT 14

Travelling the River Amazon

My name is Paco. I travel the Amazon River selling bananas. My dog, Macapa, travels with me.

The Amazon, which flows through the jungles of Peru and Brazil, carries more water than any other river in the world. It can be very dangerous for a small boat, but I've known this part of the river all my life. Everything I see tells me something. The floating leaves tell me where to paddle my boat as they follow the fastest current. This shows me where the water is deepest, so if I follow the leaves I know I will not hit a sandbank. You can't learn where the sandbanks are because they move during the rains.

I can tell a storm is coming because the wind is making waves. My little boat tips and Macapa falls in the river. I try to catch him but the current carries him away, but Macapa is a clever dog and a strong swimmer and makes for the shore, knowing I will follow him.

The sky turns purple. Lightning lights up the jungle. When we reach the bank we look for shelter. The birds and animals, sensing danger, are silent. Suddenly thunder breaks the silence, and wind roars through the jungle, bending the trees. Torrential rain hits the canopy of leaves high above us, making a noise like stones falling on a tin roof.

The storm ends as suddenly as it began. I look around in the dim light. I can't see the trees of the canopy, but I can

hear the macaws and parrots up there making noise. Below the canopy are palm, rubber and fig trees in which monkeys and tree frogs are hiding. On the floor of the forest, bushes and vines grow. White ants are chewing the wood of fallen trees.

Macapa and I head for the river. I paddle the boat as he watches the fish. There are more than 1500 kinds of fish in the Amazon, the most famous of which are the piranhas. They can eat the flesh from any mammal within minutes, but some people still swim, bathe and wash their clothes in the river. They say piranhas aren't dangerous if you keep moving.

There are electric eels that can knock you out, and the largest snake in the world, the anaconda, also lives in the Amazon. They attack people and other mammals; they even eat small cows that graze along the river banks.

Soon Macapa and I reach the market. I sell my bananas and paddle towards home. It's very hot. I want to swim in the river. First I beat the water with a stick. This stirs up the mud and scares away the animals that live in the river. I don't want to be dinner for an anaconda. I'd rather sell more bananas in Manaus tomorrow.

COMPREHENSION SKILLS

A

1 Paco paddles his boat along the River ______.

2 Macapa, his dog, is a ______ swimmer.

3 Paco earns his living by selling ______.

4 The largest snake in the world is the ______.

B Write a sentence to answer each question.

1 How does Paco know a storm is coming?

2 What happens when the birds and animals sense danger?

3 How would you feel about swimming in the River Amazon?

4 Which creature would you fear most if you were Paco?

LANGUAGE SKILLS

Comparatives

When we compare two people or things we often add **er** to the adjective. This is called the **comparative** form of the adjective.

Examples:	**adjective**	**comparative**
	deep	deep**er**
	fast	fast**er**

If the adjective ends in **y**, then we usually need to change the **y** to **i** before we add **er**.

Examples:	**adjective**	**comparative**
	sunny	sunn**ier**
	flimsy	flims**ier**

Copy these adjectives. Next to each one write its comparative.

1 busy	**2** heavy	**3** dirty	**4** mighty
5 noisy	**6** pretty	**7** dusty	**8** lively

Adding 'more'

If the adjective is a long word, and doesn't end in **y**, then instead of adding **er** we usually write **more** in front of it.

Copy these sentences, but change the adjectives to comparatives. The first is done to help you.

1 Paco says his river gets (beautiful) each day.

Paco says his river gets **more** beautiful each day.

2 The river is (turbulent) in the middle than at the side.

3 Paco's new boat is (reliable) than his old one.

4 Piranhas are (dangerous) than most fish.

'tion' suffix

Look
Cover
Remember
Write
Check

The **tion** suffix is a common ending, so words with this pattern are well worth learning. Here are some to get you started. Notice what happens to the **e**.

Examples:	create, crea**tion**	educate, educa**tion**
	situate, situa**tion**	operate, opera**tion**
	observe, observa**tion**	relate, rela**tion**

The **shun** sound at the end of a word is nearly always spelt with **tion**, not with **sh**, except in 'fashion' and 'cushion'.

A 1 Find some more **tion** words to add to your collection.

2 Learn six **tion** words. Ask a friend to test you when you are sure you know them.

B Match a **tion** word to each of these definitions.

1 close family member
2 carried out by surgeons
3 feeling
4 making something
5 provided by teachers
6 pictures in the mind
7 polite request
8 looking carefully

WRITING SKILLS

Conversations

Remember, 'new person – new line'.

When we write what is said when people are speaking to each other, it is helpful to the reader if we start a new line each time another person speaks.

Example:

"When will you be back?" asked the old man.

"Tomorrow morning," answered Paco.

"Good, I'll come to meet you then," said his old friend.

A Write this passage, adding the missing punctuation marks. Begin a new line when someone different speaks.

Will you take me for a ride on your boat? said Jose. Yes, you can come with Macapa and me tomorrow replied Paco. Where will we be going? he asked. We will take this fruit to market said Paco. Thank you Paco, that will be great said the boy excitedly.

B Write a conversation between you and a friend. You are talking about going to market tomorrow. Make it interesting for your readers.

Check-up 2

VOCABULARY

A Find these words in a dictionary.
Write their *definitions*.

magic koala perform rectangle

B Find the four word families in the box.
Write them in four lists.

collection	happily	short	colourless
unhappy	collectable	colour	shortly
colouring	shortage	happy	collected
happiest	shorter	collect	colourful

C Choose a word from each box which can be joined together to make a compound word.

thunder	note	some	screw	every	tooth

times	ache	storm	body	driver	paper

D Copy these contractions.
Next to each write out the words in full.
Like this:

1 it's = it is **2** don't **3** we've **4** haven't
5 doesn't **6** he's **7** weren't **8** they've

E Write the contractions for these words. Like this:

1 should not = shouldn't **2** would not
3 I will **4** is not
5 they are **6** will not
7 has not **8** she is
9 I am **10** he will
11 were not **12** there is
13 could not **14** did not

PUNCTUATION AND GRAMMAR

A Write these sentences. Put in the missing capital letters and punctuation marks.

1 janu emma and steven are going to see a film

2 can i come too asked errol

3 yes you can they all said

4 errol asked what time will we get home

B Copy this passage.
Add all the capital letters and punctuation marks.

can i stay up late tonight said martha no replied her father martha was cross why not she asked we are going to see your grandmother with jane ali and uncle joe tomorrow and you need to get up early in the morning said dad

C Write five adjectives to describe this child.

D Write these sentences. Underline all the active or 'doing' verbs in red and the 'being' verbs in blue.

1 I am too hot to play any more.

2 I was told to be home early.

3 We will be shouted at!

4 Mum is probably worried about us.

E Copy these sentences. Underline the subject and circle the verb in each one.

1 Nadim walked to school.

2 The rain fell on the children.

3 The children hung their coats on the pegs.

4 The coats soon dried.

F Copy the sentences from Exercise E above.
Underline the subject in red and the predicate in blue.

SPELLING

A Write the plural of these words.

1 toy = toys	4 fly	7 tray
2 key	5 story	8 baby
3 day	8 berry	9 party

B Choose **s** or **es** to make the plural of these words.

1 cat	4 arch	7 church
2 bus	5 brush	8 fox
3 horse	6 finger	9 six

C Copy this table. Fill in the missing words.

swim	swimming	swimmer
run	____	____
____	____	winner
jump	____	____
row	____	____

D Make a **tion** word from each of these words, like this:
relate, rela**tion**

1 act	3 select	5 operate
2 elect	4 educate	6 calculate